DO THE WORK!
CLEAN WATER
AND SANITATION

T0062298

COMMITTING TO THE UN'S SUSTAINABLE DEVELOPMENT GOALS

JULIE KNUTSON

CHERRY LAKE PRESS

Published in the United States of America by Cherry Lake Publishing Group
Ann Arbor, Michigan
www.cherrylakepublishing.com

Reading Adviser: Beth Walker Gambro, MS, Ed., Reading Consultant, Yorkville, IL
Photo Credits: © avijit bouri/Shutterstock.com, cover, 1; © David Talukdar/Shutterstock.com, 5; Infographic
From The Sustainable Development Goals Report 2020, by United Nations Department of Economic and Social
Affairs © 2020 United Nations. Reprinted with the permission of the United Nations, 7; © Dennis Diatel/
Shutterstock.com, 9; © PradeepGaurs/Shutterstock.com, 10; © Hari Mahidhar/Shutterstock.com, 13;
© clicksabhi/Shutterstock.com, 14; © keantian/Shutterstock.com, 15; © Kekyalyaynen/Shutterstock.com, 16;
© Mike Laptev/Shutterstock.com, 17; © Arina P Habich/Shutterstock.com, 19; © BrunoGarridoMacias/
Shutterstock.com, 20; © aapsky/Shutterstock.com, 23; © Warren Parker/Shutterstock.com, 24;
© Sergprophoto/Shutterstock.com, 27

Cherry Lake Press is an imprint of Cherry Lake Publishing Group.

Library of Congress Cataloging-in-Publication Data
Names: Knutson, Julie, author.
Title: Do the work! : clean water and sanitation / by Julie Knutson.
Description: Ann Arbor, Michigan : Cherry Lake Publishing, 2022. | Series: Committing to the UN's sustainable
    development goals | Audience: Grades 4-6
Identifiers: LCCN 2021036386 (print) | LCCN 2021036387 (ebook) | ISBN 9781534199286 (hardcover) |
    ISBN 9781668900420 (paperback) | ISBN 9781668901861 (pdf) | ISBN 9781668906187 (ebook)
Subjects: LCSH: Sustainable development—Juvenile literature. | Environmental ethics—Juvenile literature. |
    Water quality—Juvenile literature. | Water—Purification—Juvenile literature.
Classification: LCC HC79.E5 K585 2022 (print) | LCC HC79.E5 (ebook) | DDC 628.1/6—dc23
LC record available at https://lccn.loc.gov/2021036386
LC ebook record available at https://lccn.loc.gov/2021036387

Cherry Lake Publishing Group would like to acknowledge the work of the Partnership for 21st Century
Learning, a Network of Battelle for Kids. Please visit http://www.battelleforkids.org/networks/p21
for more information.

Printed in the United States of America
Corporate Graphics

The content of this publication has not been approved by the United Nations and does not reflect the views of the
United Nations or its officials or Member States. For more information on the Sustainable Development Goals please visit
https://www.un.org/sustainabledevelopment.

ABOUT THE AUTHOR

Julie Knutson is an author-educator who writes extensively about global citizenship and the
Sustainable Development Goals. Her previous book, *Global Citizenship: Engage in the Politics
of a Changing World* (Nomad Press, 2020), introduces key concepts about 21st-century
interconnectedness to middle grade and high school readers. She hopes that this series will
inspire young readers to take action and embrace their roles as changemakers in the world.

TABLE OF CONTENTS

CHAPTER 1

Meet the SDGs

It's a hot summer day, and you've just come inside after a long bike ride. You shuffle to the kitchen sink, turn on the faucet to pour a glass of water, and . . . nothing. Hoping to cool down, you try the shower. That's dry too. The sprinkler outside? No luck there either.

This might seem like something that would never really happen. But for residents of water-stressed cities, there's a real danger of the pipes running dry in the future. Already, half of the world's population experiences severe water scarcity for at least 1 month each year. With a growing global population, climate instability, and shrinking **aquifers**, concerns about water security are increasing around the world. It's predicted that two-thirds of the world's population will face water stress by 2025.

Handwashing is a major way to prevent diseases.

STOP AND THINK: *We constantly use water, often without thought. Keep a water log for 1 day. When and how do you use water? How would your life be different if water wasn't so readily available?*

It's not just water supply—water quality is also a concern. Access to clean and safe drinking water, as well as access to water for sanitation and hygiene, is an issue in many areas. In 2017, 785 million people lacked access to basic drinking water services. Three billion people didn't have a simple hand washing station with soap and water at home. The impact? Preventable deaths caused by contaminated water and poor sanitation conditions.

What Are the SDGs?

In 2015, the **United Nations** (UN) released the 17 **Sustainable** Development Goals (SDGs). The SDGs range from "Zero Hunger" (SDG 2) to "Reduced Inequality" (SDG 10) to "Life on Land" (SDG 15). At the core, these 17 goals are about making life better now and in the future for "people and the planet." All 191 UN member states have agreed to cooperate in reaching the 197 SDG targets by 2030.

With SDG 6, the UN sets out a goal for "Clean Water and Sanitation" by 2030. The promise of SDG 6 is to "ensure availability and sustainable management of water and sanitation for all."

Why Is Water So Important?

The world's first civilizations were built along riverbanks. That's no accident—fresh water is necessary for both people and businesses to survive. Later societies, like the ancient Romans and the Maya, used water to grow into thriving empires. Even today, 90 percent of the world's population lives within 6.2 miles (10 kilometers) of a freshwater source.

6 CLEAN WATER AND SANITATION

ENSURE AVAILABILITY AND SUSTAINABLE MANAGEMENT OF WATER AND SANITATION FOR ALL

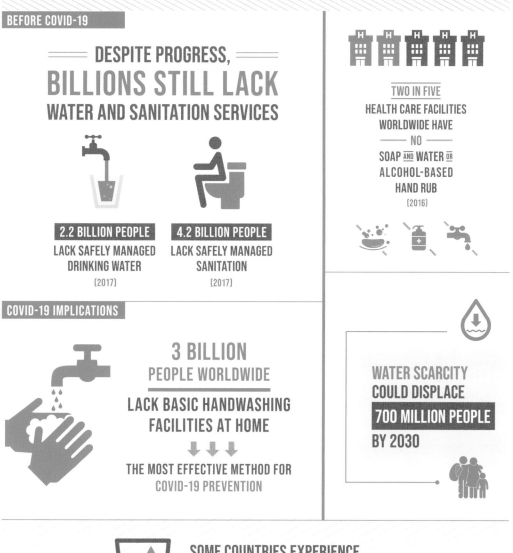

BEFORE COVID-19

DESPITE PROGRESS, BILLIONS STILL LACK WATER AND SANITATION SERVICES

2.2 BILLION PEOPLE
LACK SAFELY MANAGED DRINKING WATER
(2017)

4.2 BILLION PEOPLE
LACK SAFELY MANAGED SANITATION
(2017)

TWO IN FIVE
HEALTH CARE FACILITIES WORLDWIDE HAVE
— NO —
SOAP AND WATER OR ALCOHOL-BASED HAND RUB
(2016)

COVID-19 IMPLICATIONS

3 BILLION
PEOPLE WORLDWIDE

LACK BASIC HANDWASHING FACILITIES AT HOME

THE MOST EFFECTIVE METHOD FOR COVID-19 PREVENTION

WATER SCARCITY COULD DISPLACE **700 MILLION PEOPLE** BY 2030

SOME COUNTRIES EXPERIENCE A FUNDING GAP OF 61% FOR ACHIEVING WATER AND SANITATION TARGETS

SUSTAINABLE DEVELOPMENT **GOALS**

Because water is so critical for survival, it's considered a basic human right. But that right isn't guaranteed to billions of people. In parts of the United States, water **utilities** are so expensive that some households spend 20 percent of their income on it. Elsewhere in the world, people have to walk miles to reach a well or lake. Some spend their entire day in the journey. These people often sacrifice other essential rights, such as the right to education. With SDG 6, **infrastructure** that improves the safety of and access to water will change the lives of billions.

Related Goals

Progress on SDG 6 will pave the way to the success of other connected goals, ranging from "Good Health and Well-Being" (SDG 3) to "Climate Action" (SDG 13). The World Health Organization (WHO) summarizes just how critical clean water is to human health and progress. WHO authors explain:

"When water comes from improved and more accessible sources, people spend less time and effort physically collecting it,

A family travels together to get water in Uganda.

Water is collected in plastic containers.

meaning they can be productive in other ways. This can also result in greater personal safety by reducing the need to make long or risky journeys to collect water. Better water sources also mean less expenditure on health, as people are less likely to fall ill and incur medical costs, and are better able to remain economically productive.

With children particularly at risk from water-related diseases, access to improved sources of water can result in better health, and therefore better school attendance, with positive longer-term consequences for their lives."

Health, education, the ability to work, and physical safety are all improved by protecting water resources and promoting sanitation. Keep reading to learn about how you can help safeguard this precious resource!

A Long Walk to Water

Linda Sue Park's book *A Long Walk to Water* describes the lives of two people in South Sudan, Salva Dut and Nya, whose experiences are separated by two decades. Separated from his family, Salva survived Sudan's civil war in the 1980s. After 10 years in **refugee** camps, he moved to New York. In the early 2000s, he learned his father was alive but was hospitalized due to a water-borne **parasite**. Salva traveled to South Sudan and launched an organization called Water for South Sudan. Since then, Water for South Sudan has drilled more than 450 wells, each of which serves 500 to 1,000 people. This has allowed children such as Nya to attend school.

CHAPTER 2

Why Do We Have Goals?

Let's say you want to learn how to do something new. Maybe it's playing the piano or learning a new language. Whatever it is, you'll want to start with a plan. That's the most achievable way to reach a goal.

Just as people set goals, so do large organizations like the UN. To reach the SDGs, the UN set specific targets and **indicators**. These ensure that the goals aren't just big ideas, but achievable aims. They also give governments and people guidelines for measuring progress and reaching the SDGs.

> STOP AND THINK: *The acronym "SMART," which stands for Specific, Measurable, Achievable, Relevant, and Timed, is often used in setting goals. Why do you think it is important for people to consider these factors when developing goals? How could they help a person or organization achieve a goal?*

A girl collects well water from a hand pump.

According to the UN, every 15 seconds, a child dies
from a preventable, water-borne illness.

Monitoring groups report that 80 percent of wastewater worldwide is dumped, untreated, into water supplies.

For SDG 6, the specific, smaller targets are:

- Safe, affordable drinking water for all.
- Create access to toilets, sanitation, and hygiene so that people no longer have to **defecate** in open, public spaces.
- Improve water quality, wastewater treatment, and safe reuse.
- Increase water-use **efficiency** and ensure freshwater supplies to make sure that future water supplies are available and protected.
- Implement **Integrated Water Resource Management**.
- Protect and restore water-related ecosystems, including **groundwater** systems.

There are over 16,000 wastewater treatment plants in the United States.

Water purification tanks at a wastewater treatment plant.

These targets will be achieved by:

- Expanding water and sanitation support to developing countries.
- Supporting local engagement in water and sanitation management.

Ready to help make these targets a reality? Keep reading to learn about what you can do at home, at school, and in the larger world to build a water-secure future!

CHAPTER 3

Do the Work! Contribute to the Goals at Home

Environmental researcher Debra Perrone, who studies water use in the western United States, points out two key factors that will shape future water security. These are finding new supplies and reducing demand. At home, you can help with the latter. Lessen your household's demand on water by taking a few simple actions.

- **Reduce Use** — Did you know that the average person in the United States uses 80 to 100 gallons (303 to 378.5 liters) of water per day? That's more than a standard bathtub, which holds about 70 gallons (265 l)! Some people use up to 2 gallons (7.6 l) of water just to brush their teeth. Be conscious of your personal water use. Take shorter showers and don't let water run in the sink. Instead of tossing ice from drinks down the drain, use it to water plants!

Turn off the tap while brushing your teeth.

A leaking tap can waste more than 3,000 gallons (11,356 l)
of water each year.

- **Educate Yourself and Others** — Encourage others in your household to take the same actions to reduce use. Remind your family members not to pour chemicals or medicine down the drain or in the toilet. Our water treatment systems aren't designed to filter out these chemicals. They can end up harming both human and fish populations.
- **Help Choose Household Products** — Basic soap and water get the job done for hand hygiene! Avoid products with **triclosan**, which is added to some soaps as an antibacterial agent. There's no benefit to using it for basic hand-washing, and some scientists believe that it can harm marine ecosystems.

CHAPTER 4

Do the Work! Contribute to the Goals at School

Think of ways you and your classmates can help! Your school is a great place to learn about different issues and create goals. Then put those goals into action by educating others!

- **Learn** — Books like *A Long Walk to Water* provide a great entry point into engaging with the topics of water scarcity and quality. Set your own questions around water issues. What would you like to learn more about? Are you interested in preventable, water-borne illnesses and global public health? Would you like to know more about water justice

Lead pipes can **corrode** and cause water to turn brown.

issues in the United States, such as **lead**-contaminated drinking water? Do you want to know about how scientists are using wastewater as a resource, or **desalinating** ocean water to make it drinkable? Follow your interests, do research, and tell others about what you've learned.

Around 40 percent of the world's population does not have access to toilets.

- **Speak Up and Educate Others** — Each year, the UN highlights water issues through special holidays and observances. March 22 is World Water Day, and November 19 is World Toilet Day. Mark these days by raising awareness about clean water and sanitation. You can make posters, write an editorial for the school newspaper, or invite a guest speaker to your class. You can also work with your school librarian to host a read-aloud and discussion for younger students. Share what you learn with family, friends, and neighbors!

What other kinds of events and discussions could be held in your school to draw attention to water issues? Brainstorm with a friend, and talk to a teacher about making your ideas a reality.

- **Fundraise** — In the afterword to the 2015 edition of *A Long Walk to Water*, Linda Sue Park and Salva Dut note "Teachers, librarians, school administrators, parents, and most especially students have raised hundreds of thousands of dollars for Salva's **nonprofit** organization, Water for South Sudan." You and your classmates can join them! In the past, student groups have held walks for water, made "wishing wells" for spare change, and created "water walls" featuring paper droplets of water that name people who have made donations. Channel your creativity to help build wells in water-stressed parts of the world!

CHAPTER 5

Do the Work! Contribute to the Goals in Your Community

What can you do to encourage others in your community to conserve, preserve, and protect this life-sustaining natural resource?

Volunteer

Research organizations in your community that protect and preserve freshwater and groundwater sources. Young people can help with volunteer water-monitoring programs and with waterway cleanups. In Colorado, seventh- and eighth-grade members of the Cheyenne Creek Conservation Club take water samples, clean up trash, plant trees, and raise awareness about pollution and stormwater runoff on local ecosystems.

Safely clean up trash along beaches and waterways.

Advocate

Be an advocate for water rights issues. Learn about water justice issues, from lead in drinking water to lack of access to water infrastructure on **Indigenous** lands. Email, write, or call politicians and ask them to pass laws ensuring that water is affordable and accessible for all people.

Lead in Drinking Water

Lead is a chemical element once used to line plumbing pipes. Over time, it can corrode and seep into drinking water. Exposure to lead can cause health and learning issues, particularly in children. In 2014, residents of Flint, Michigan, battled to get state authorities to recognize that their water was tainted with lead. It took nearly 2 years for officials to address how bad this environmental crisis was.

Lead isn't just a problem in Flint. A 2019 study of American schools showed "a pattern of widespread contamination of drinking water." According to this government study, just 43 percent of school districts test for lead. Of the sites tested, one-third had elevated lead levels. Experts recommend guidelines requiring all schools to test for lead and replacing water fountains that contain lead. They also urge installing and maintaining filters on faucets used for cooking and drinking.

[21ST CENTURY SKILLS LIBRARY]

Extend Your Learning

Understanding Groundwater Pollution

Aquifers are natural storage containers for water that lies deep belowground. Water has accumulated in these groundwater sources for thousands of years. The largest aquifer in the United States is the High Plains Aquifer, which covers about 174,000 square miles (450,658 square kilometers) in the central plains.

Around the world, people dig wells to extract water from aquifers. But at the current rate, people are using water faster than nature can replenish it. Runoff from human waste also makes its way into these groundwater deposits. To understand how this process works and why groundwater should be protected, create your own model of an aquifer. Follow along with this activity from the Aquarium of the Pacific: *https://www.aquariumofpacific.org/downloads/IAFTM_AquiferLesson.pdf.*

Further Research

BOOKS

Gilles, Renae. *Clean Water in Infographics.* Ann Arbor, MI: Cherry Lake Publishing, 2021.

Knutson, Julie. *Flint Water Crisis.* Ann Arbor, MI: Cherry Lake Publishing, 2021.

Labrecque, Ellen. *Clean Water.* Ann Arbor, MI: Cherry Lake Publishing, 2018.

WEBSITES

Goal 6: Ensure Access to Water and Sanitation For All—
United Nations Sustainable Development
https://www.un.org/sustainabledevelopment/water-and-sanitation
Check out the UN's Sustainable Development Goals website for more information on Goal 6.

The Global Goals of Sustainable Development
margreetdeheer.com/eng/globalgoals.html
Check out these free comics about the UN's Sustainable Development Goals.

World Health Organization: Drinking Water
www.who.int/news-room/fact-sheets/detail/drinking-water
Check out the World Health Organization's information on drinking water.

Glossary

aquifers (AH-kwuh-fuhrs) rock layers that contain water

corrode (kuh-ROHD) to destroy or damage by a chemical action

defecate (DEH-fih-kayt) to expel feces

desalinating (dee-SAH-luh-nay-ting) process of removing salt from ocean or seawater

efficiency (ih-FIH-shuhn-see) producing desired effects with no waste of energy

groundwater (GROWND-wah-tuhr) water held underground in the soil or in open areas in rock

indicators (in-duh-KAY-tuhrs) measurements of progress

Indigenous (in-DIH-juh-nuhss) native to a place

infrastructure (IN-fruh-struhk-chuhr) basic physical and operational needs for society to operate, such as roads and bridges

Integrated Water Resource Management (IN-tuh-gray-tuhd WAH-tuhr REE-sohrss MAH-nij-muhnt) coordinating the development and management of water and land resources to promote sustainability

lead (LED) a metallic element that can cause severe damage when breathed in or eaten

nonprofit (nahn-PRAH-fuht) an organization that does not seek to make a profit

parasite (PAIR-uh-syte) an organism that lives off and takes energy and nutrients from another organism

refugee (REH-fyoo-jee) a person who has been forced to flee their country because of war, natural disaster, or persecution

sustainable (suh-STAY-nuh-buhl) able to be maintained at a certain rate

triclosan (trih-KLOH-sahn) a chemical often added to household products to kill bacteria and fungi

United Nations (yuh-NYE-tuhd NAY-shuhns) the international organization that promotes peace and cooperation among nations

utilities (yoo-TIH-luh-teez) organizations supplying the community with electricity, gas, water, or sewerage

INDEX